Pennycook Elementary School
3620 Fernwood Street
Vallejo, CA 94591
707-556-8590

LIGHTNING BOLT BOOKS™

What Do We Buy?

A Look at Goods and Services

Robin Nelson

Lerner Publications Company
Minneapolis

To Zach and Maren, my favorite consumers of goods and services

Lerner Publications Company
A division of Lerner Publishing Group, Inc.
241 First Avenue North
Minneapolis, MN 55401 U.S.A.

Website address: www.lernerbooks.com

Library of Congress Cataloging-in-Publication Data

Nelson, Robin, 1971–
        What do we buy? : a look at goods and services / by Robin Nelson.
            p. cm. — (Lightning bolt books™—Exploring economics)
        Includes index.
        ISBN 978-0-7613-3913-7 (lib. bdg. : alk. paper)
        1. Consumer goods—Juvenile literature. 2. Service industries—Juvenile literature.
    3. Production (Economic theory)—Juvenile literature. 4. Consumption (Economics)—Juvenile
    literature. I. Title.
    HF1040.7.N45 2010
    339.47—dc22   2009027470

Manufactured in the United States of America
1 — BP — 12/15/09

Contents

What Do You Buy?

Have you ever bought sticky, sweet cotton candy? Have you ever paid to have a colorful rainbow painted on your cheek?

Cotton candy is a good. The face painter is providing a service. Everything that is bought or sold is a good or a service!

This woman is painting a design on the boy's face.

Goods

Goods are things you can touch. Food, clothes, and toys are goods. Look at all the goods in a toy store!

This toy store sells many goods.

A marble is a good. When you use money to buy marbles, you are buying goods.

Mmmmm! Yummy pizza!

When you buy a pizza, you are buying a good. Goods are everywhere!

Services

Services are jobs that people do for others. A teacher, a plumber, and a server in a restaurant provide services.

This plumber is fixing the sink.

You can buy services. When your bike breaks, you take it to the shop to get it fixed. When it is fixed, you pay the shop money. You are buying a service.

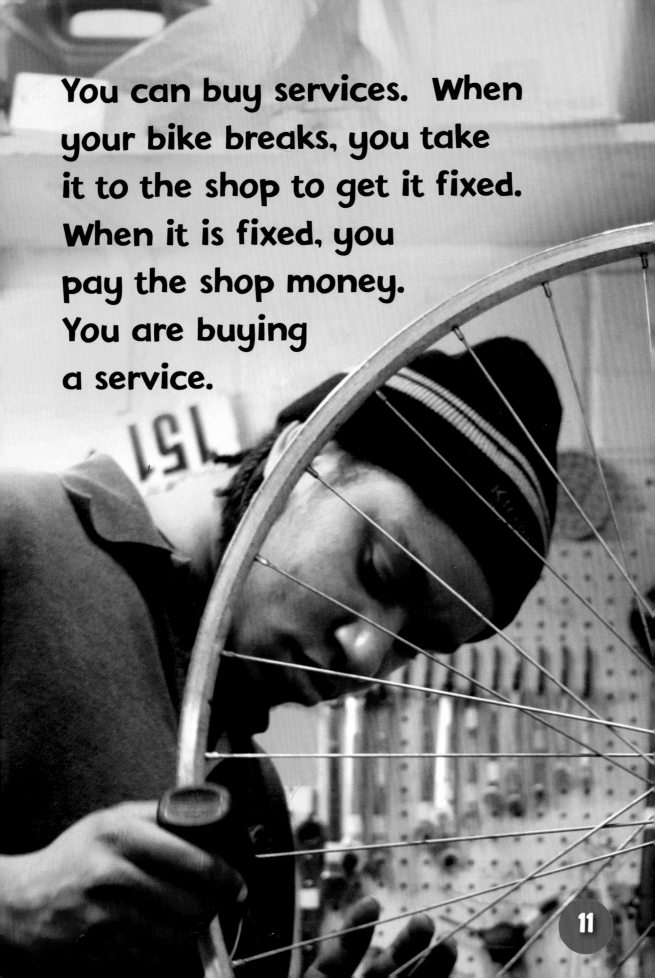

Some services create goods. A cook in a restaurant provides the service of cooking a hamburger and french fries for you to eat.

The hamburger and french fries are goods. When you give the restaurant money, you are paying for both goods and services.

These women are paying for goods and services at a restaurant.

13

Needs and Wants

Some goods and services are things you need. A need is something you must have.

A bed is a need. On cold nights, a blanket is a need too!

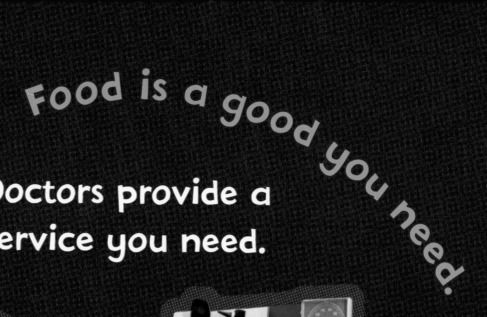

Food is a good you need.

Doctors provide a service you need.

Some goods and services are things you want. A want is something you would like to have.

A video game is a good you want. Toys and music are wants too.

A haircut is a service you want. (Well, it's a service your mom wants!)

Consumers and Producers

Did you know that you are a consumer and a producer?
A consumer is someone who buys or uses goods and services.

These boys are consumers. They're buying candy.

You are a consumer when you buy a new toy. You are a consumer when you listen to your teacher read a book.

A producer is someone who makes goods or provides services. You are a producer when you make cookies for a bake sale.

You are a producer
when you wash
your mom's car.

21

Resources

To make goods and provide services, we need resources.

Resources are things we use to create goods and services.

These cleaning supplies are resources. The girl needs them to do her chores.

Natural resources come from nature. The sun, trees, and water are natural resources.

These crops are growing in a field. They need plenty of sun and water.

Human resources are the people who do work.

Builders, teachers, and scientists are human resources.

These workers are building a house.

Capital resources are goods made by people to make other goods or services.

A hammer, a tractor, and a computer are capital resources.

Workers use hammers to build houses. A hammer is a capital resource.

Resources make goods and services all around you.

Fruits and vegetables grow on farms. This woman sells them at a farmers market.

What goods and services do you buy?

What Do You Want to Be?

What job do you want when you grow up? Will you provide a good or a service? Ask friends what they would like to be. Will they provide goods or services? Make a chart from their answers.

What Do You Want to Do When You Grow Up?

Make a Good	Provide a Service
Emily: make video games	Me: be a doctor
Nicholas: be a baker	Alexis: be a famous singer
Derrick: be an artist	Chris: be a baseball player
Abby: write books	Sofia: be an astronaut
Jacob: make movies	Josh: teach kids
Akira: make cars	Karah: be a firefighter
	Daniel: own a toy store

Quiz:
Good or Service?

Which of these photos show someone providing a service? Which photos show a good?

Answers are on page 31.

Glossary

capital resource: a thing created by people to make goods and services

consumer: someone who buys or uses goods and services

good: a thing you can touch that is bought or sold

human resource: a person who works to create goods and services

natural resource: a thing that comes from nature and is used to create goods and services

need: something you must have

producer: someone who makes goods or provides services

resource: a thing used to create goods and services

service: work done by someone for others

want: something you would like to have

Further Reading

Andrews, Carolyn. *What Are Goods and Services?*
New York: Crabtree, 2009.

Houghton, Gillian. *Goods and Services.* New York:
PowerKids Press, 2009.

It's My Life: Money
http://pbskids.org/itsmylife/money/index.html

Larson, Jennifer S. *Who's Buying? Who's Selling?:*
Understanding Consumers and
Producers. Minneapolis: Lerner
Publications Company, 2010.

Roberson, Erin. *All About*
Money. New York: Children's
Press, 2004.

Answer key for page 29:
Goods: hat and gloves, camera, shoes
Services: farmer, doctor, firefighter

Index

Photo Acknowledgments

The images in this book are used with the permission of: Reflexstock/Corbis RF/Randy Faris, p. 2; © James P. Blair/CORBIS, p. 4; © iStockphoto.com/Isabel Masse, p. 5; © Tanya Constantine/Blend Images/Getty Images, p. 6; © Todd Strand/Independent Picture Service, p. 7; © iStockphoto.com/Danny Hooks, p. 8; © iStockphoto.com/Lisa F. Young, p. 9; © iStockphoto.com/Catherine Yeulet, pp. 10, 27; © Steve Skjold/Alamy, p. 11; © Eric Futran-Chefshots/Foodpix/Getty Images, p. 12; © RIA/Novosti/TopFoto/The Image Works, p. 13; Reflexstock/Corbis RF/C) Brooke Fasani/ p. 14; © Rob Melnychuk/ Getty Images, p. 15; © iStockphoto.com/rarpia, p. 16; © iStockphoto.com/sonyae, p. 17; © White Packert/Iconica/Getty Images, p. 18; © Kablonk!/Photolibrary, p. 19; © iStockphoto.com/iofoto, p. 20; © Sinibomb Images/Alamy, p. 21; Reflexstock/ Rubberball/Mike Kemp, p. 22; © Claver Carrol/Photolibrary, p. 23; © Lester Lefkowitz/ Stone/Getty Images, p. 24; © iStockphoto.com/Peter Austin, p. 25; © Julie Caruso, p. 26; © iStockphoto.com/Michael Krinke, p. 29 (top left); © iStockphoto.com/Leslie Banks, p. 29 (top center); © iStockphoto.com/Neustockimages, p. 29 (top right); © iStockphoto.com/Christoph Weihs, p. 29 (bottom left); © iStockphoto.com/Carlos Alvarez, p. 29 (bottom center); © iStockphoto.com/Jason Lugo, p. 29 (bottom right); © Sean Justice/Riser/Getty Images, p. 30; Reflexstock/cultura RF/Dave & Les Jacobs, p. 31.

Front cover: © Julie Caruso/Independent Picture Service.